The Story of MENCIUS

www.royalcollins.com

Picture Story Book of
Ancient Chinese Thinkers

The Story of MENCIUS

Li Weiding
Translated by Wu Meilian

RC
Books Beyond Boundaries
ROYAL COLLINS

Picture Story Books of Ancient Chinese Thinkers
The Story of MENCIUS

Li Weiding
Translated by Wu Meilian

First published in 2024 by Royal Collins Publishing Group Inc.
Groupe Publication Royal Collins Inc.
550-555 boul. René-Lévesque O Montréal (Québec) H2Z1B1 Canada

ISBN: 979-8-9852490-4-0

To find out more about our publications, please visit www.royalcollins.com.

From his childhood, when he moved three times with his mother, to his old age, when he lectured and wrote, Mencius lived a rich and magnificent life.

His daily life with his mother solidified his belief in seeking knowledge.

His travels to various countries, his words and debates, and his firm ideals governing the country are all part of Mengzi's life.

Standing beside Mencius in the painting, observing his expressions, listening to his words, and observing his actions, one can feel the lofty and advancing life attitude of the "Second Sage."

One can also sense his profound and vast intellectual wisdom.

More than 2,400 years ago, there were hundreds of vassal states, large and small, scattered across the land that is today's China. In addition to the seven major States of Qin, Chu, Qi, Yan, Han, Zhao, and Wei, there were also many others, such as the States of Song, Lu, Zheng, Wei, Xue, Teng, and Zou. For more than 200 years, the larger states often fought and attacked each other to compete for land and annex smaller states. Therefore, this era is referred to as the "Warring States Period."

In addition to wars, this time period also received its name from the frequent arguments and debates among scholars who belonged to various schools of thought, such as Confucianism, Mohism, Names, Legalism, Agriculturalism, and Yin-Yang. These scholars had to elaborate and promote their own thoughts and strategies for governing the country and participating in politics.

On April 2, 372 BCE, the fourth year of King Lie of Zhou, a boy was born in the Meng family in the Fu Village in the State of Zou. His name was Meng Ke, and he would grow up to become the great thinker Mencius.

To support the family, little Meng Ke's father had to work away from home all year round, and the heavy responsibility of caring for and educating his son fell on Meng's mother alone.

The Meng family lived next to the cemetery. Whenever there was a funeral, little Meng Ke would go and join in for fun, and soon, he began to imitate funeral rituals when playing: digging holes, burying things, kneeling, and crying. When his mother saw this, she thought this was not something her son should learn, so she decided to move.

They moved to a bustling market with many shops. Little Meng Ke started to play trading games with his new friends, shouting and bargaining. His mother felt that this environment was not conducive to her child's growth, so she moved again.

This time, they moved next to a school. Every day, the students studied the etiquette of offering to their ancestors and meeting with the lords and kings. Seeing little Meng Ke also learning these behaviors, his mother happily settled here.

Meng Ke's mother worked hard as a weaver to supplement the family income and support her son's studies. One day, little Meng Ke hurried home after school finished without saying goodbye to the teacher. His mother asked, "How is your study?"

Meng Ke replied, "It's still the same as before."

Hearing this, his mother picked up scissors and cut off the cloth she was weaving. Little Meng Ke was very frightened and asked why she did this. The mother said, "You are neglecting your studies, just like I am cutting off the cloth on this loom. To weave a piece of cloth, I must do it with every single thread inch by inch. The same is true with studying. Learning is not something that happens in a day or two. If you give up halfway and stop at a superficial level, how can you achieve something great in the future?"

After that day, Meng Ke studied diligently, day and night.

When he was fifteen or sixteen years old, Meng Ke became the disciple of Confucius' grandson, Zisi, and studied Confucius's teachings. He began to form his understanding of the world around him, believing the feudal lords were profit-driven with their internal wealth accumulation and external aggression. Su Qin and Zhang Yi's strategies only contributed to the ongoing chaos. No one's theory of that time was worth learning. Only Confucius' teaching was correct.

At the age of thirty, Meng Ke became an accomplished scholar, and he began to give lectures to apprentices and form his own ideological system and political opinions in this process. His goal was to carry forward the teachings of the sage Confucius, to change this world of decline and chaos, and to create a benevolent and righteous world.

As the number of his disciples increased and his influence grew, he became known as Master Meng or Mencius. After Duke Mu of the State of Zou heard about him, he summoned Mencius to inquire about the way of governing the country. Mencius was forty years old when he visited Duke Mu and shared his political opinions with him.

A conflict broke out between the States of Zou and Lu, and many Zou officials sacrificed their lives to defend the city. The people of Zou, however, did not offer any help but watched them die.

Duke Mu of Zou was very angry about this and asked Mencius how he should punish the people. Mencius said, "In years of famine, the king's treasury and granary were full. The people were starving to death in the wilderness, but no officials reported their sufferings to the king. How do you expect the people to save the officials in times of war? They will only be close to officials and willing to sacrifice for them when they are treated with kindness during peacetime."

While Mencius was in Zou, his official career did not make much progress. When his father died of illness, he could only afford the cheapest coffin. He buried his father according to scholar-bureaucrats etiquette with the offerings of beef, fish, and bacon carried in three *ding* vessels (a ritual vessel for cooked food with a round body and three legs).*

Three years passed in mourning, and Mencius still saw no hope of achieving his political aspiration in the State of Zou. Therefore, he left his home country with his disciples to advocate the ideal of benevolent governance in other countries. Their journey lasted more than twenty years.

Mencius made the State of Qi his first destination. During Duke Huan's reign, the Jixia Academy in Linzi, the capital of Qi, attracted scholars from various schools of thought where they could write books and discuss politics. During King Wei's time, the Jixia Academy became even more prosperous.

---

* The "system of ranking by *dings*" was stipulated in the ritual system of the Zhou Dynasty: the Son of Heaven (king) used nine *dings*, the feudal lords used seven *dings*, the ministers used five *dings*, and scholar-bureaucrats used three *dings* or one *ding*.

For a long time after Mencius arrived in Qi, he was not taken seriously by King Wei of Qi. Despite his high position, his idea of "benevolent ruling" could not be accommodated by Qi's existing Legalist policies. He was thus often worried.

One day, Mencius was at home, grieving about his situation. His mother heard him sigh and asked why he was sad. Mencius said, "A gentleman should accept a position according to his heart's desire. He must not accept unfair rewards, not be greedy for vanity, not give advice if his ideas are not accepted, and not set foot in the court if his ideas are not implemented. Now that the King of Qi did not adopt my advice, I wish to leave and go to another kingdom, but I worry that you could not endure the hardships of the journey."

His mother replied, "The virtue of a woman lies in taking care of the household. They should obey their father at home, obey their husband when married, and obey their son after the husband dies. You are a man now, and you should act according to your own wishes. I am old now, but I will follow your will." Nevertheless, Mencius was still concerned about his mother's health and did not travel.

The next year, Mencius' mother passed away. Mencius was very sad, and he carefully arranged her funeral with exquisite quilts and a fine wood coffin made by himself. After the funeral, Mencius sent his mother back to the State of Lu for burial in her ancestral grave. He used five *ding* vessels to offer her sacrifices of lamb, pork, cut meat, fish, and bacon according to the etiquette of ministers, and he observed mourning for three years.

Mencius had been in Qi for six or seven years, and he no longer had any expectations for King Wei. With no concerns after his mother passed away, Mencius chose to leave and pursue his dream in another kingdom. He decided to go to the State of Song because King Yan of Song was hoping to implement a benevolent government.

Wan Zhang asked Mencius, "A small country like Song wants to implement the benevolent ruling, but it causes the two big kingdoms of Qi and Chu to hate and attack it. What should we do?" Mencius replied with a confident smile, "As long as the King of Song can truly implement benevolent governance, he will win support from all people of the world. What does he have to fear even if Qi and Chu are powerful?"

However, soon after arriving in the State of Song, Mencius discovered that there were too few wise men around the king. The villains gathered around him as soon as the virtuous man left, so it was too difficult to implement benevolent ruling here. Similarly, when a man from Chu wanted his son to learn the Qi dialect, it would be too difficult if the boy was still influenced by Chu people around him every day.

In desperation, Mencius asked for his resignation from the King of Song, who gave him seventy *yi** of gold as travel expenses. When passing by the State of Xue, the King of Xue also gave Mencius fifty *yi* of gold to buy weapons for self-defense. Finally, after a long and rough journey, Mencius returned to his hometown. He was already over fifty years old at this time.

---

* *Yi* is an ancient Chinese weight measurement, and one yi equals about 1200 g.

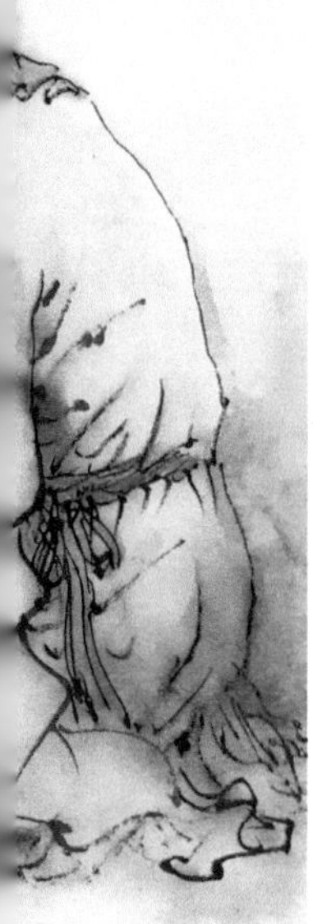

More than ten years had passed since he left home. Both his parents were no longer around, and his ideals were still not realized. Fortunately, he had many disciples with him at this time. Some only studied with Mencius for a short period before they moved to various places, but they often came back to visit him and ask him for advice.*

* Mencius had many disciples, including Yuezheng Ke, Gongsun Chou, Wan Zhang, Gongdouzi, Chen Zhen, Chong Yu, Xianqiu Meng, Chen Dai, Peng Geng, Wulu Lian, Tao Ying, Xu Pi, and Meng Zhongzi.

A man from the State of Ren asked Wulu Lian, "Which is more important, etiquette or food?"

Wulu Lian replied, "Etiquette is more important."

The man asked again, "If you look for food according to etiquette, you will starve to death, but you will not starve if you don't follow the etiquette. In this case, is etiquette still important?"

Wulu Lian was at a loss and didn't know how to answer.

The next day, he made a special trip to the State of Zou to visit his teacher, Mencius. Mencius said, "If you don't measure the height of the foundation but just compare the ends, a one-inch-long wooden block can be taller than a tall building with a spire. Gold is heavier than feathers, but what about a whole cart of feathers compared to one small gold coin? There is no standard answer to many questions, but people must learn to identify the priority of a situation."

Yuezheng Ke was a kind and devoted student, and Mencius liked him very much. When Duke Ping of Lu appointed Yuezheng Ke as a court official, Mencius was so happy that he could not sleep.

Gongsun Chou asked, "Is Yuezheng Ke strong, strategic, and well-learned?"

"No," said Mencius, "he is good at taking in honest advice."

Gongsun Chou asked again, "Is this enough?"

Mencius replied, "Of course. If you are willing to listen to good advice, people from all over the world will come to offer it to you. You will grow and improve with all the wisdom and honesty in the world, then will it be difficult for you to govern the country?"

After Yuezheng Ke came to power, he recommended his teacher to Duke Ping of Lu. On this day, a favored minister, Zang Cang, met the Duke on his way out and said, “Usually, when Your Highness goes out, the officials would know the travel destination. Today, the carriages and horses are ready, but we do not know where Your Highness is going, so I come to ask.”

Duke Ping replied: “I’m going to visit Mencius.”

Zang Cang stopped him and said, “How can Your Highness condescend to visit an ordinary person? Is Mencius a virtuous man? The funeral he held for his mother was much larger than his father’s. Is this what a virtuous man should do? Your Highness must not go see him.”

The Duke believed in Zang Cang’s words and did not visit Mencius.

Hearing this, Yuezheng Ke paid an audience with Duke Ping and explained, "When Mencius was a scholar, he used three *ding* vessels to worship his father; later, when he became a high official, he used five *ding* vessels to worship his mother. There is nothing wrong with that."

Duke Ping said, "I am talking about the burial clothes and the coffin."

Yuezheng Ke replied, "That is only because of the difference in his financial status before and after."

Later, Yuezheng Ke told Mencius about Duke Ping's planned unsuccessful visit, and Mencius said, "The Duke's visit is beyond human control. It is Heaven that prevents me from meeting with the Duke of Lu. How can a petty minister influence this situation?"

When Duke Wen of Teng (in modern-day Shandong Province) was still the prince, he visited Mencius twice, learning about the stories of legendary kings Yao and Shun and the principle that human nature is inherently good. After Mencius returned to the State of Zou, Duke Wen sent Ran You to ask twice about the etiquette of his father's funeral. Therefore, Mencius believed that Duke Wen understood the etiquette well. After Duke Wen came to the throne, he invited Mencius to come to the State of Teng, providing him with a high-quality residence and a large guard of honor consisting of dozens of carriages and hundreds of servants when he went out.

Duke Wen of Teng highly respected Mencius's opinions and often asked him for advice on how to govern the country.

Mencius suggested, "Implement the well-field system and give the people a stable career to make them feel at ease; reduce levy taxes so that the people will be rich; set up schools to teach ethics and morals, and the people will care for each other and support their king; forced labor should not conflict with the farming season to affect production, and the country will naturally be stable and prosperous."

But Teng was a small state, and its most urgent concern was foreign invasion. When the neighboring State of Xue was destroyed, and the State of Qi sent troops to reinforce its city walls, Duke Wen felt seriously threatened. Mencius's suggestions failed to address the most important needs of the country and were inconsistent with the contemporary social situation.

Although Mencius's plan failed to gain stability in the State of Teng, his influence and reputation increased significantly, and many scholars often came to visit him.

When Yi Zhi of the Mohist school came, Mencius did not meet with him the first time, excusing himself for being sick. Yi Zhi came again, and Mencius said, "The Mohists advocate for simple funerals, but you held luxurious funerals for your parents. Isn't that treating your parents in ways that you despise?"*

---

* Mohism, established by Mo Di, was one of the schools of thought in the Warring States Period. It upheld concepts of "universal love," "worshipping the wise," "anti-extravagant burial rituals," "anti-invasion," "heaven with self-will," and "worshipping spirits and ghosts," which had a deep influence on the society then.

Yi Zhi answered, "The ancient kings cared for their people as they cared for infants, which means that there is no difference in affection between people, whether they are close or distant."

Mencius said, "You equalize compassion with indiscriminate love, but every person has only one origin, and that is their parents."

Yi Zhi thought about it and said, "Thank you for your words."

Xu Xing, an Agriculturalist, came to Teng with dozens of disciples from Chu. They wore coarse linen clothes and made a living by weaving straw sandals and mats.

Chen Xiang, a disciple of Confucian Chen Liang, also arrived in Teng with his younger brother from Song. After meeting Xu Xing, he was very happy, so he abandoned all his previous learning and studied with Xu Xing.

Later, during a visit to Mencius, Chen Xiang asked a question on Xu Xing's behalf, "The Duke of Teng does not farm with the people but asks the people to support him. How can he be considered wise?"

Mencius asked, "Did Xu Xing knit his own hat? Did he make the pots for cooking and the iron tools for plowing the fields by himself?"

Chen Xiang answered, "No."

Mencius continued, "The labors in a society must be divided. Some people work with their minds, and some with their strength. If you ask everyone to produce before using anything, then everyone will be exhausted. If rough and exquisite shoes are sold at the same price, who will make exquisite shoes anymore? How can society progress in this way?"

The State of Liang was a big and powerful state that was in constant wars with the States of Qi, Qin, and Chu to expand its territory. King Hui of Liang lost not only some of his cities but also his eldest son. In his later years, King Hui sought out talented people with humble etiquette and generous treatment to improve the country's situation. For example, when the Yin-Yang philosopher Zou Yan came to Liang, King Hui went to the outskirts to greet him and treated him as a distinguished guest. However, when Mencius arrived afterward, he was not treated the same way.

King Hui of Liang asked Mencius, “Old sir, you have come all the way; what benefits can you bring to my state?”

Mencius answered, “Why do you only talk about interests? Let us just talk about benevolence and righteousness. People who care about interests will not be satisfied. If everyone in a country is competing for interests, the country will be in danger because the scholar-bureaucrats will try all they can to seize the king’s property. Only those who value benevolence and righteousness will not abandon their parents or disrespect their king.”

One day, King Hui was standing by the pool and admiring the scenery in the garden. The geese were soaring in the forest, and the elk foraging by the water. Everything was fine and peaceful. Seeing Mencius, the king asked, "Did the ancient sages also enjoy this kind of happiness?"

Mencius replied, "The benevolent King Wen of Zhou built the Lingtai platform and the Lingzhao pond; his people were happy, and so were the birds and fish; the evil King Jie of Xia also built high platforms and deep pools, but his people wanted nothing but his death, even if it cost their own lives. Only virtuous people can enjoy this kind of happiness!"

King Hui of Liang had never accepted his failures in wars. "My country is big and powerful, but I was defeated by the States of Qi, Qin, and Chu one after another. It was so humiliating. How could I avenge for my people who died in wars?" he asked.

Mencius answered, "If you implement benevolent ruling with less punishment and taxes, if the young people are filial towards their fathers and elder brothers and respectful and loyal to their superiors, then your people can defeat the armies of Qi and Chu even with wooden sticks. As the old saying goes, 'The benevolent are invincible.' "

After many talks with Mencius, King Hui's admiration for him grew enormously. Unfortunately, the king died the second year after Mencius arrived in Liang.

His son, King Xiang of Liang, came to the throne. After Mencius paid an audience with King Xiang, Mencius sighed and thought to himself, "He does not look like a king from a distance, and I cannot see his majesty up close. When he talks to me, his words are completely inconsistent."

Mencius felt that his staying in Liang was pointless, so he decided to go to the State of Qi. The new King Xuan of Qi had recently succeeded to the throne and was implementing changes in laws. Mencius met King Xuan when passing through Fan County and thought him quite majestic by his look. He sighed, "A person's living environment can change his qualities; a person's diet and nourishment can affect his appearance. The influence of the environment is truly significant!"

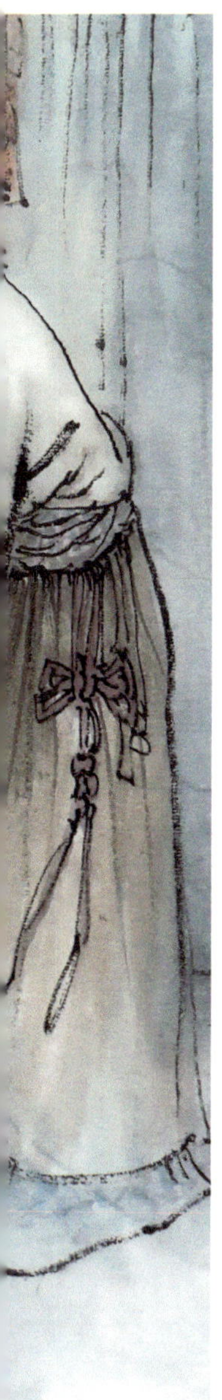

King Xuan was very curious about this famous thinker and sent people to spy on Mencius' daily life to see how he was different from others. After Mencius learned about it, he smiled and said, "What difference can there be? Even the ancient sages Yao and Shun are no different from ordinary people!"

On this day, Mencius was about to go to see King Xuan. The king sent a messenger who said, "His Majesty originally wanted to come to see you, but unfortunately, he caught a cold. If you go see him, he will receive you at court. Are you willing to have an audience with His Majesty?" After hearing this, Mencius said to the envoy, "Unfortunately, I have also caught a cold and cannot go to court."

The next day, Mencius went to Mr. Dongguo's house to attend a mourning ceremony. Gongsun Chou advised him, "You just declined King Xuan's summons yesterday on the pretext of being ill. Maybe you should not go to the mourning so quickly."

Mencius said, "I was sick yesterday, but I'm fine today. What's wrong with that?"

As soon as Mencius went out, the king sent a messenger and a doctor to visit him. Meng Zhongzi told the visitors, "Mencius was sick yesterday when he received His Majesty's summons, but he is feeling better today, and he has set off for the court. I don't know if he has arrived now." As soon as the envoy left, Meng Zhongzi hurriedly sent someone to stop Mencius on his way home and told him, "You must not go home. Go to court quickly."

Mencius had no choice but to hide in Jing Chou's house. "The king seems to respect you very much, but why don't you respect His Majesty?" asked Jing Chou.

Mencius explained, "There are three things that are recognized as noble in the world: title, age, and morality. In the court, the title is most important; in society, age is most important; as for assisting the monarch and ruling the people, morality is most important. How can His Majesty disrespect my age and morals because of his authority? There are ministers a monarch must approach to seek advice but cannot summon if he wishes to achieve something great. It is not worth serving him if the king does not sincerely believe in benevolence and righteousness."

On the outskirts of Linzi, there is a palace called the Snow Palace, with gorgeously decorated pavilions and gardens raising various rare animals. King Xuan summoned Mencius to this place and asked, "Do benevolent people also have this kind of happiness?"

Mencius replied, "Yes. If not, they will complain about the monarch. It is wrong for the people to complain about the monarch when they do not have something, but it is even wrong for a monarch not to enjoy the same things as the people. There has not been such a case in which a king was unloved by the people when he shared the worries and joys of the people."

King Xuan asked again, "I heard that King Wen of Zhou's Garden was about seventeen miles in length and width. Was it true?"

Mencius replied, "This is recorded as such in the history books."

King Xuan continued, "My garden is only ten miles in length and width. Why do people consider it big?"

Mencius replied, "Although King Wen's Garden was large, people could enter it to collect hay and firewood and to hunt birds and hares. But anyone who kills an elk in Your Majesty's Garden is punished for the same crime as murdering a person. How can people not consider the garden big?"

When Duke Wen of Teng passed away, King Xuan of Qi sent Mencius to pay his respects with an arrogant senior official, Wang Huan (courtesy name Zi'ao), to assist him. On their way, Wang Huan would meet with Mencius twice a day, but Mencius never discussed the mission with him. Gongsun Chou was puzzled, so Mencius explained, "Why should I talk about it if the business is already taken care of?"

Another time, when official Gongxingzi held the funeral for his son, Wang Huan came to express his condolences. As soon as he entered the door, everyone went to greet him, but Mencius ignored him. Wang Huan was very unhappy and said, "All the officials came to talk to me, but only Mencius was rude to me."

After hearing this, Mencius said, "According to etiquette, in the court, you cannot talk to the person over the person next to you, and you cannot bow after you cross the stairs. I treated him with etiquette, but Zi'ao thought I was being rude. Isn't it strange?"

In 316 BCE, King Kuai of the State of Yan gave up the throne to Prime Minister Zizhi and never took part in political affairs from then on. In the second year, Prince Ping and General Shi Bei tried to seize power but failed for several months, and they were eventually killed by Zizhi.

King Xuan of Qi wanted to take the opportunity to annex the State of Yan, so he sent General Kuang Zhang to attack Yan. Kuang Zhang captured the capital city in fifty days and killed Zizhi.

After the victory, the Qi army not only killed and robbed innocent people in Yan, but also destroyed the Yan State's ancestral temples. The other states began to discuss sending troops to rescue Yan. King Xuan asked Mencius what he should do. Mencius advised him to discipline the Qi soldiers, stop the killing and plundering, select a new king for Yan with the Yan people's consent, and withdraw the Qi troops. However, King Xuan did not adopt Mencius's suggestion.

Two years later, with the help of other states, the new King Zhao of Yan came to the throne and defeated the Qi army. King Xuan regretted his failure and said, "I cannot face Mencius now."

While King Xuan was feeling ashamed, Mencius felt disappointed about King Xuan and decided to leave Qi. King Xuan went to see Mencius in person and tried to persuade him to stay, to which Mencius could only answer, "I hope we can meet again."

A few days later, King Xuan said to the official Shizi, "I want to give Mencius a house in the capital and support his disciples to live well in Qi, so that the people in our country can follow their examples and learn about Confucianism. Why don't you talk to Mencius for me?"

Shizi met with Mencius and expressed King Xuan's request. Mencius said, "If I want to get rich, why should I resign my post that could provide me ten times more of what His Majesty pays me out of pity?"

Mencius stayed for a night in Zhou County, and someone there wanted to retain Mencius for King Xuan. The person spoke to Mencius respectfully, but Mencius did not pay attention to him and even dozed off on the table.

The man was very unhappy, "I fasted for a day before I dared to talk to you, but you refuse to listen. I will never dare to see you again."

Mencius said hurriedly, "If I can't win the King's respect and appointment but only stay for his provision, how do you expect an old man like me to live?"

Mencius stayed in Zhou County for three days, hoping that King Xuan would call him back. But the king's message never came.

Mencius embarked on his return journey with great sorrow and reluctance. On the way, his disciple Chong Yu asked, "Didn't you say in the past that a gentleman does not complain about his environment and others?"

Mencius said, "The time has changed. Every 500 years, a sage king would appear with virtuous ministers to assist him. It has been 700 years since the Zhou Dynasty; who should it be other than our generation to help bring peace to the world?" The melancholy Mencius ended his traveling and returned to his hometown. The State of Qi was both the starting and end points for his journey.

Mencius, now in his sixties, concentrated on teaching after returning to the State of Zou. He and some of his disciples compiled remarks on arguments and questions during his travels into seven chapters, known as *Mencius*, to pass down his thoughts to future generations.

On November 15, 289 BCE, the twenty-sixth year of King Nan of Zhou, the great Confucian thinker Mencius passed away at the age of eighty-four. His thoughts have influenced the entire Chinese nation to this day.

ABOUT THE AUTHOR

Li Weiding (1956–2018) was a Chinese painting and comic artist. He was the vice president of Shanghai Wenhui Calligraphy and Painting Academy, a national first-class artist, and a member of the Artists Association. His representative works include traditional Chinese paintings such as *Figures in Old Shanghai Stone Gate Houses* and *Poetry and Painting Collection*, as well as comic works such as *The Old Horse Knows the Way* and *Ouyang Xiu*, which won the first prize in the Third National Comic Book Set Competition.